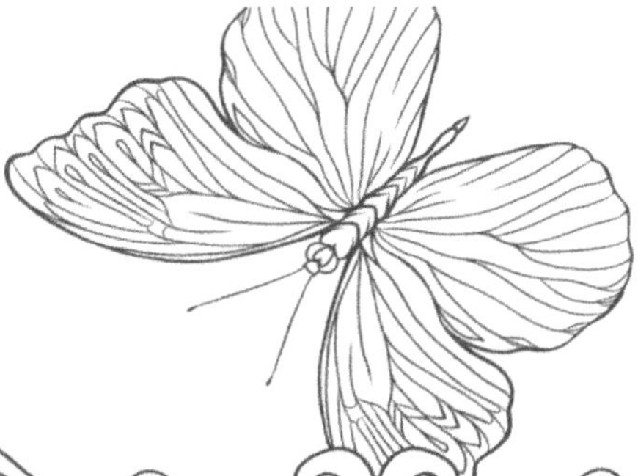

This book is belongs to

_____

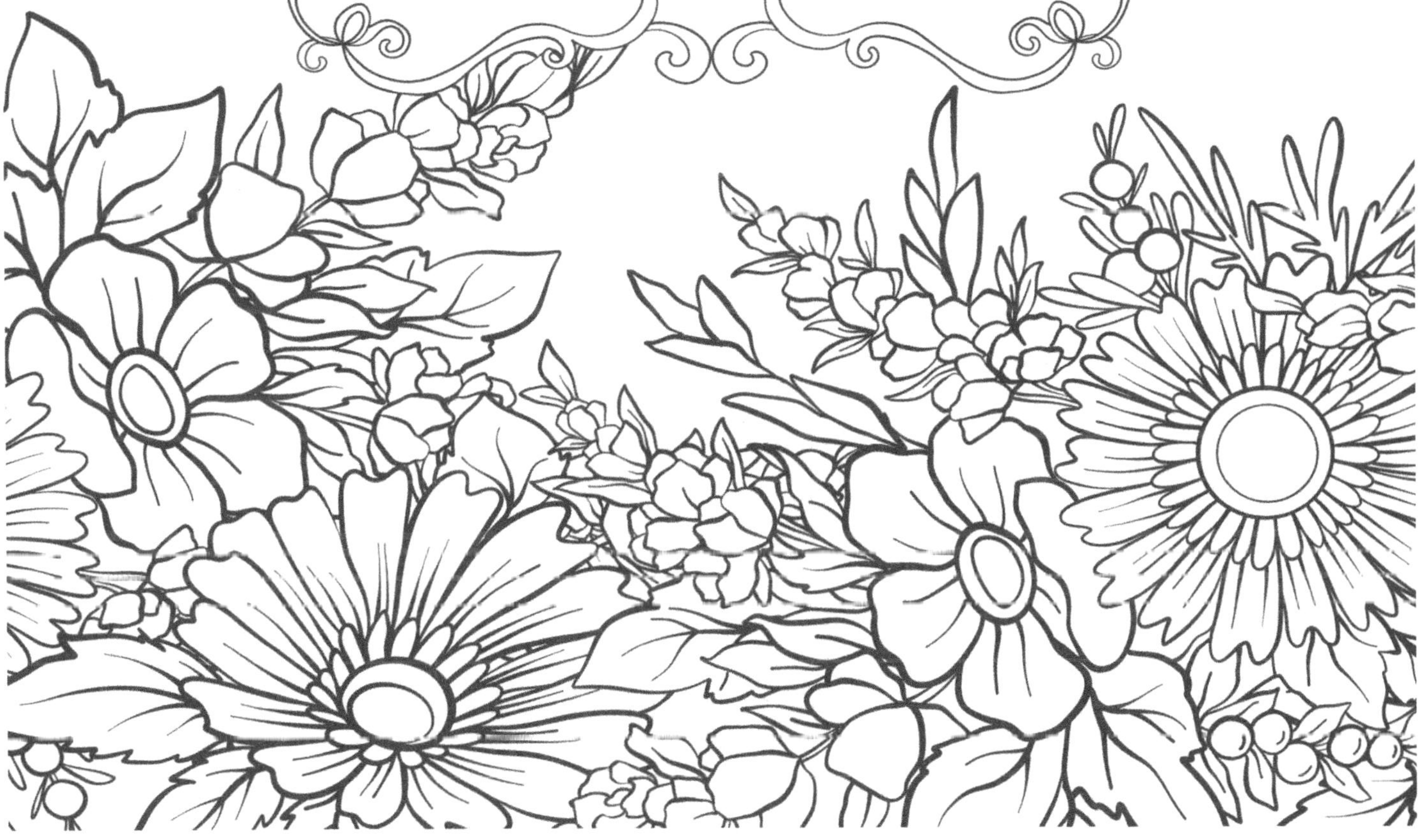

Panista Publishing

I0481421

Color Test PaGe

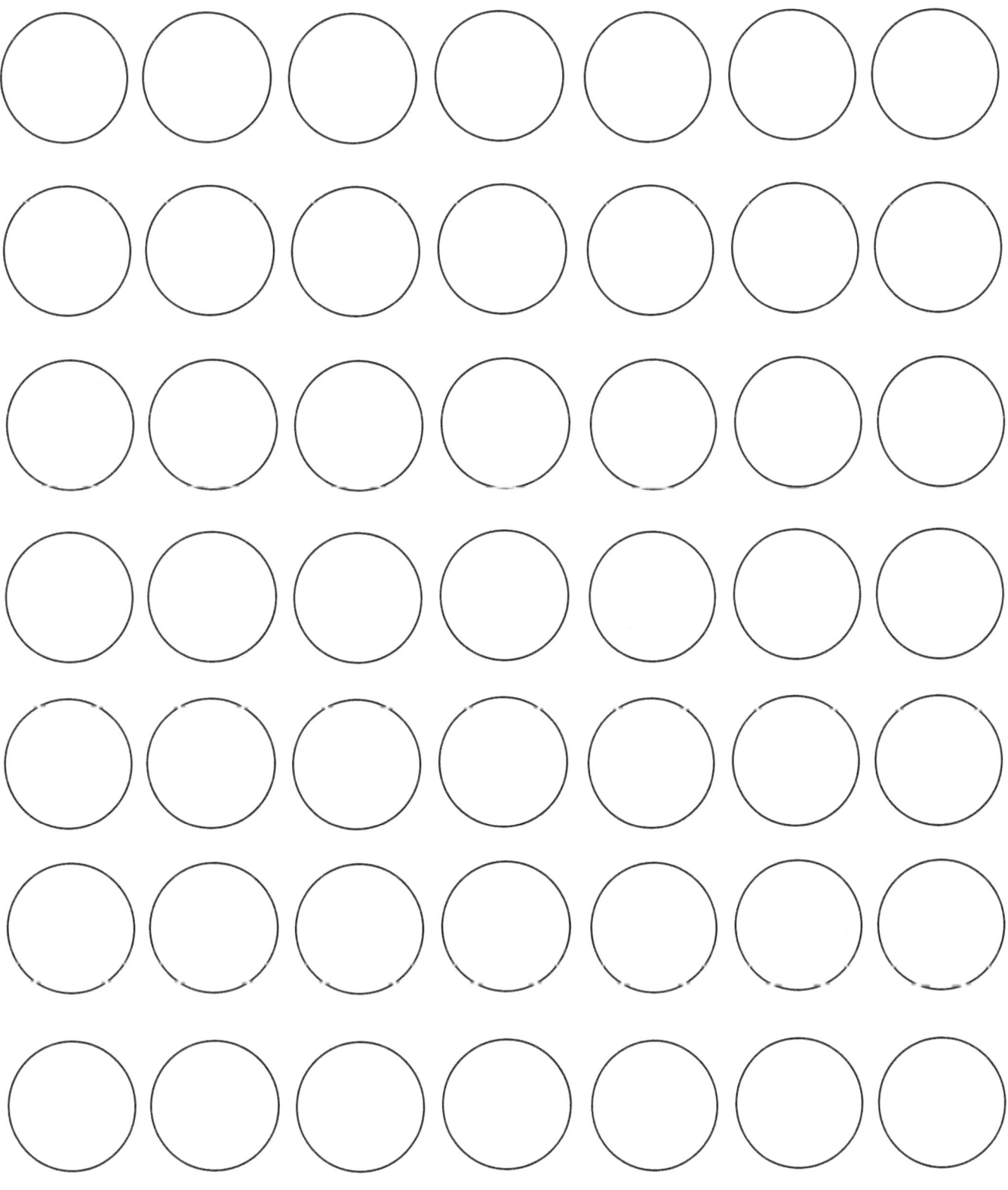

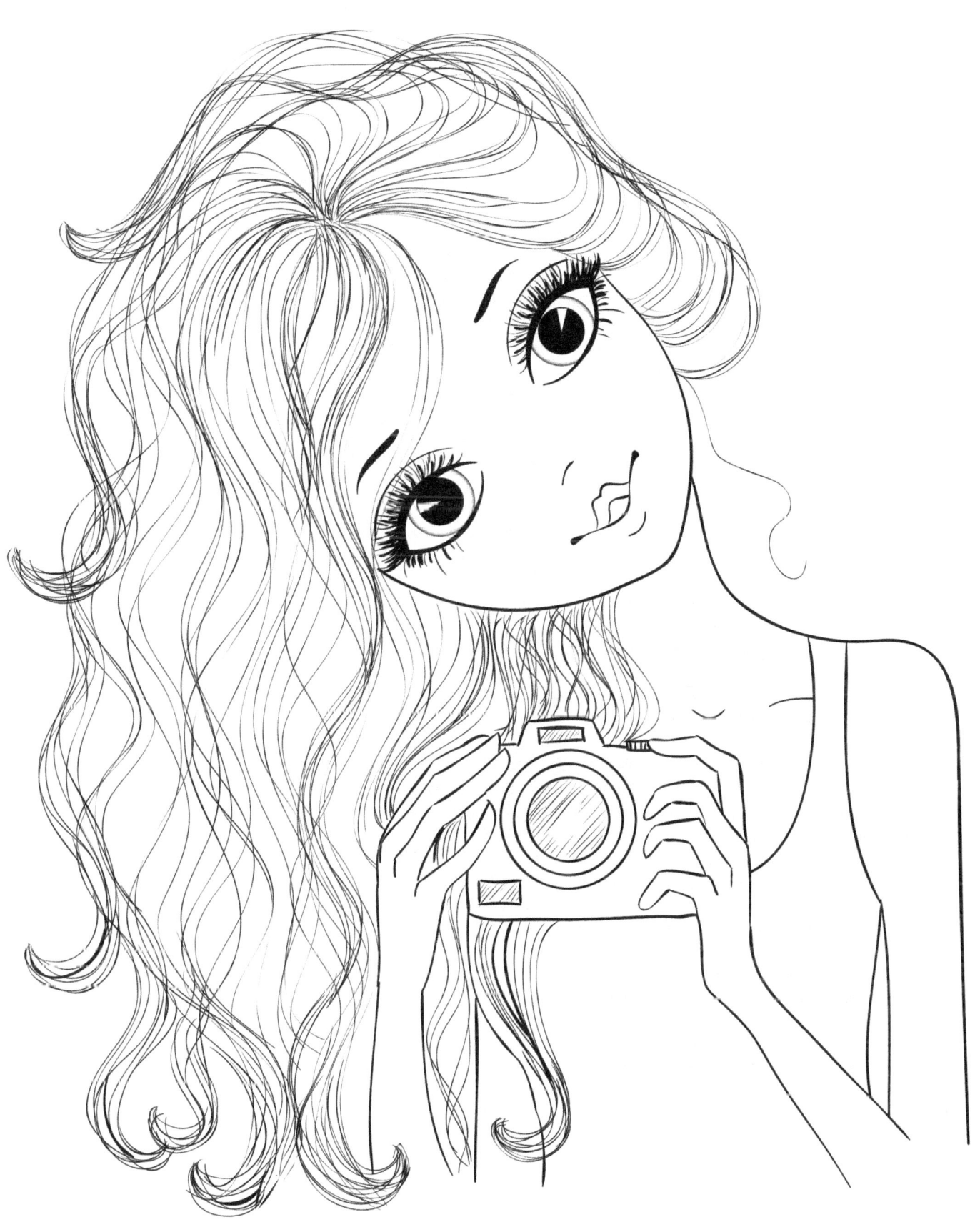

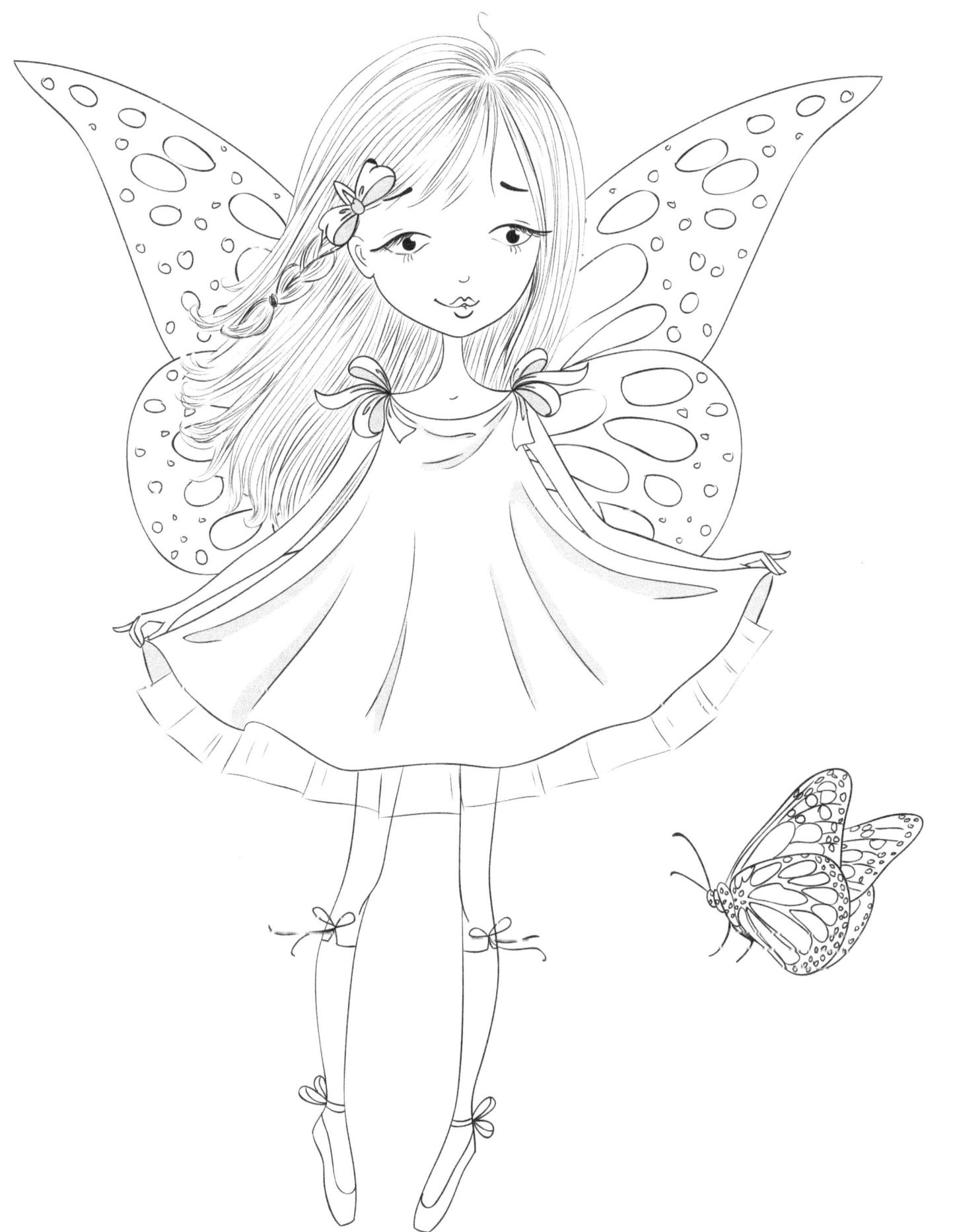

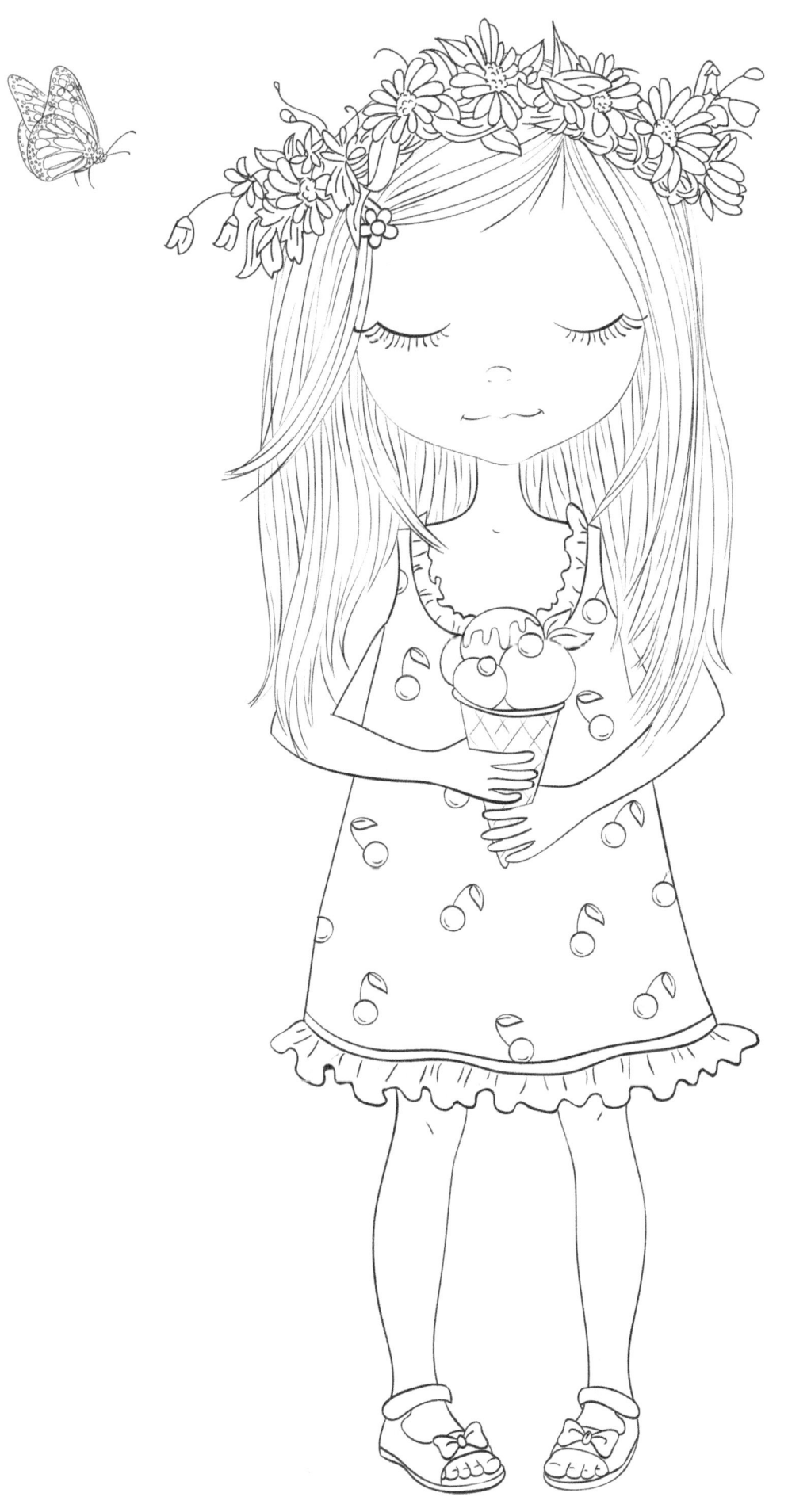

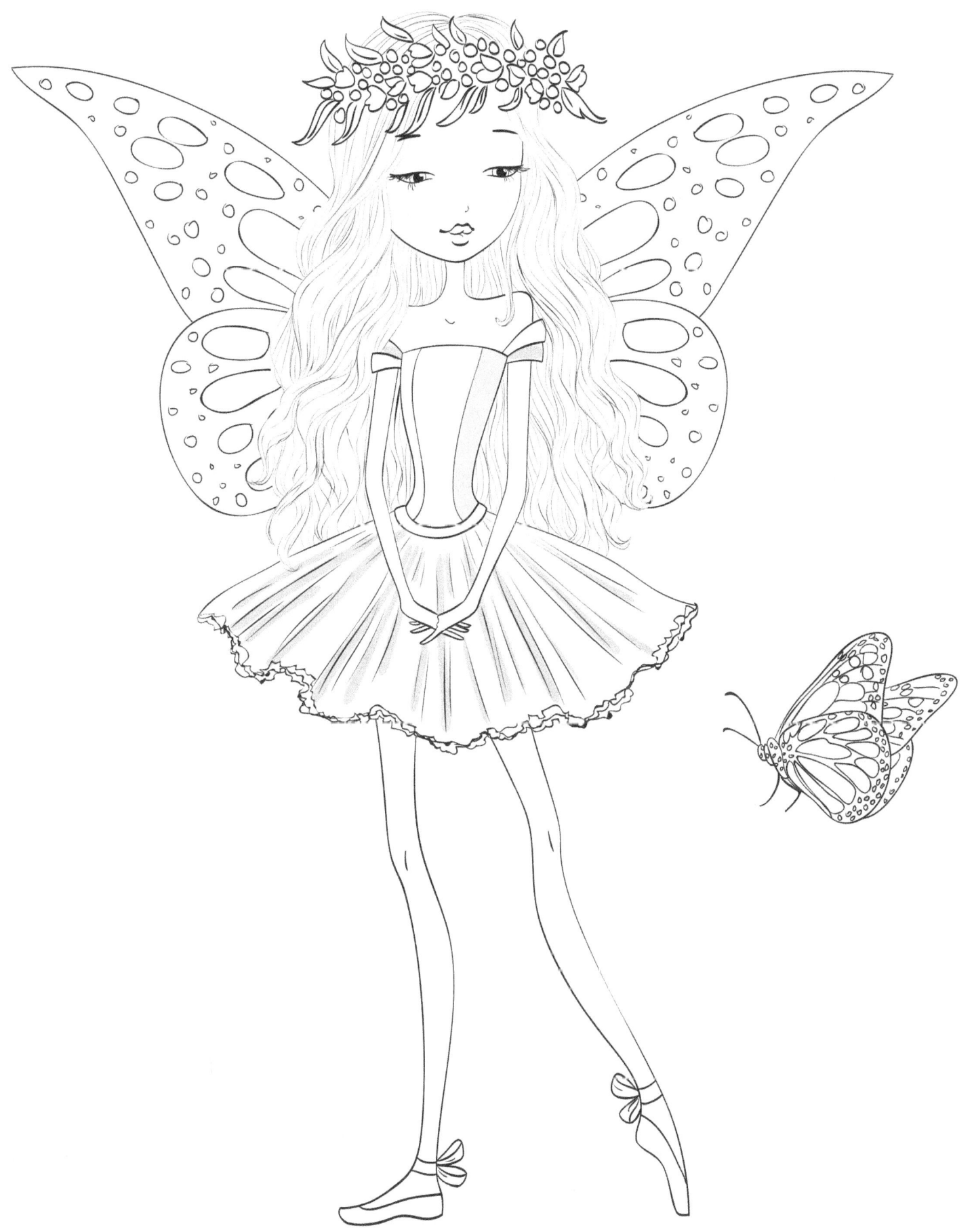

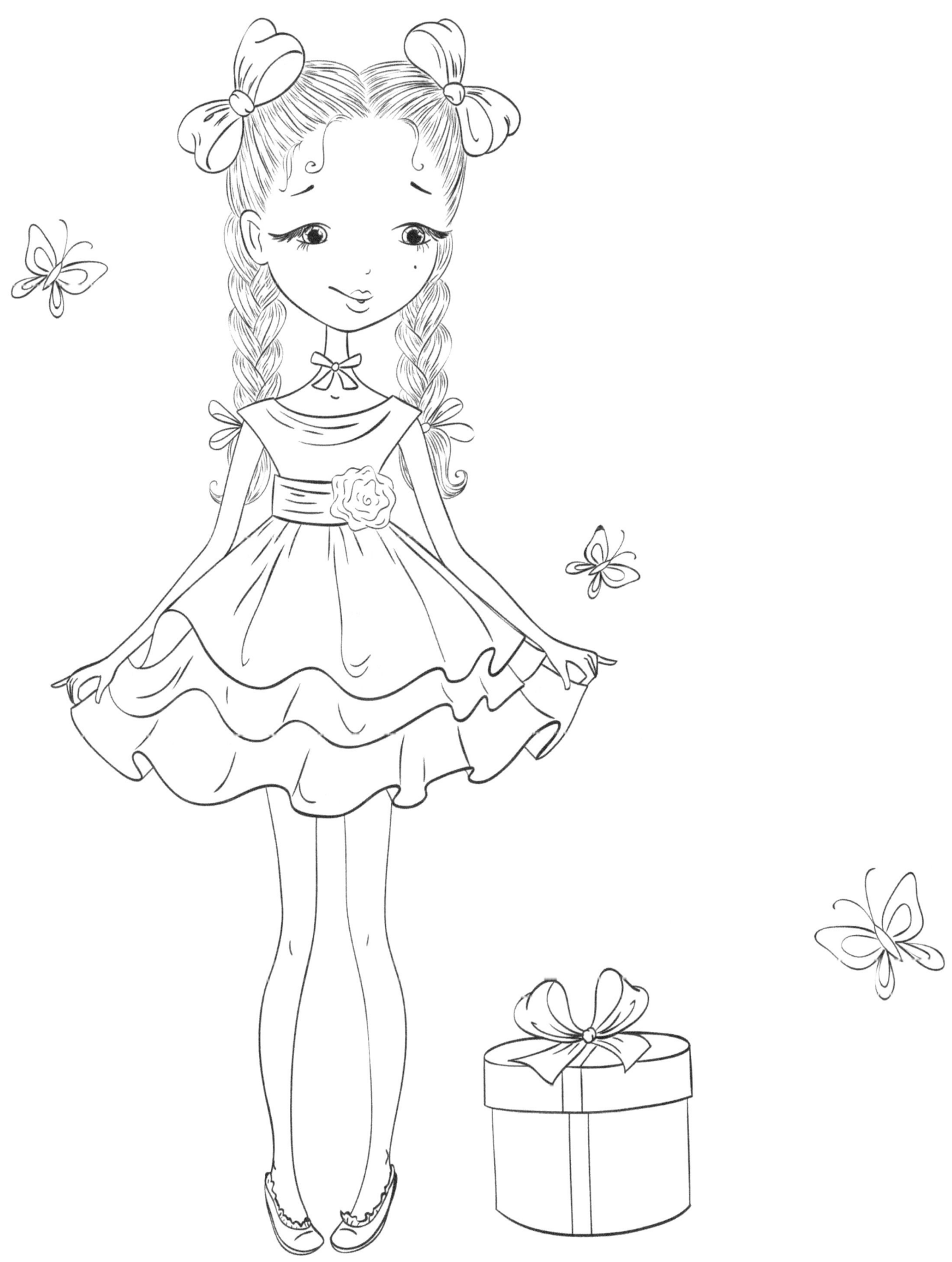

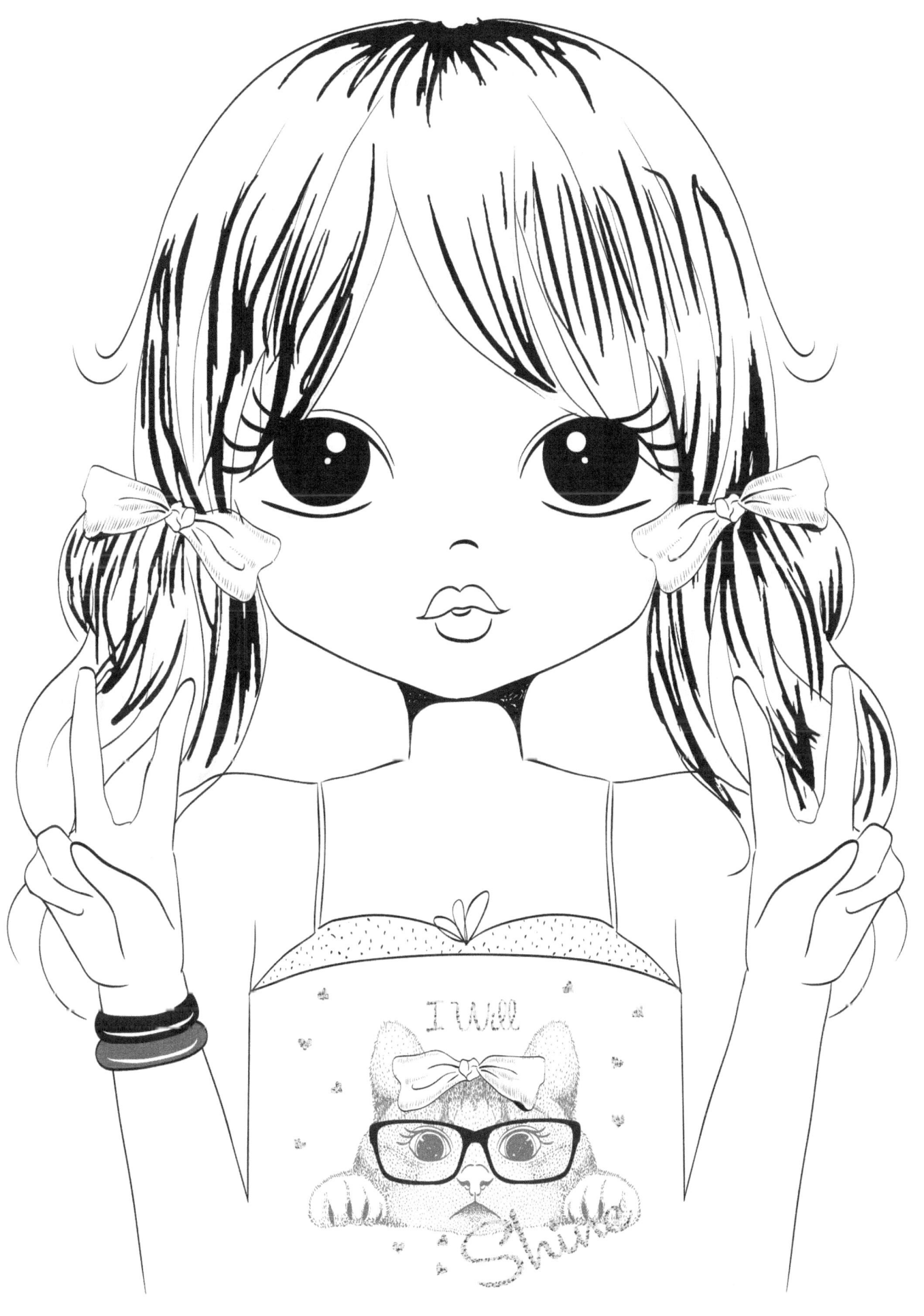

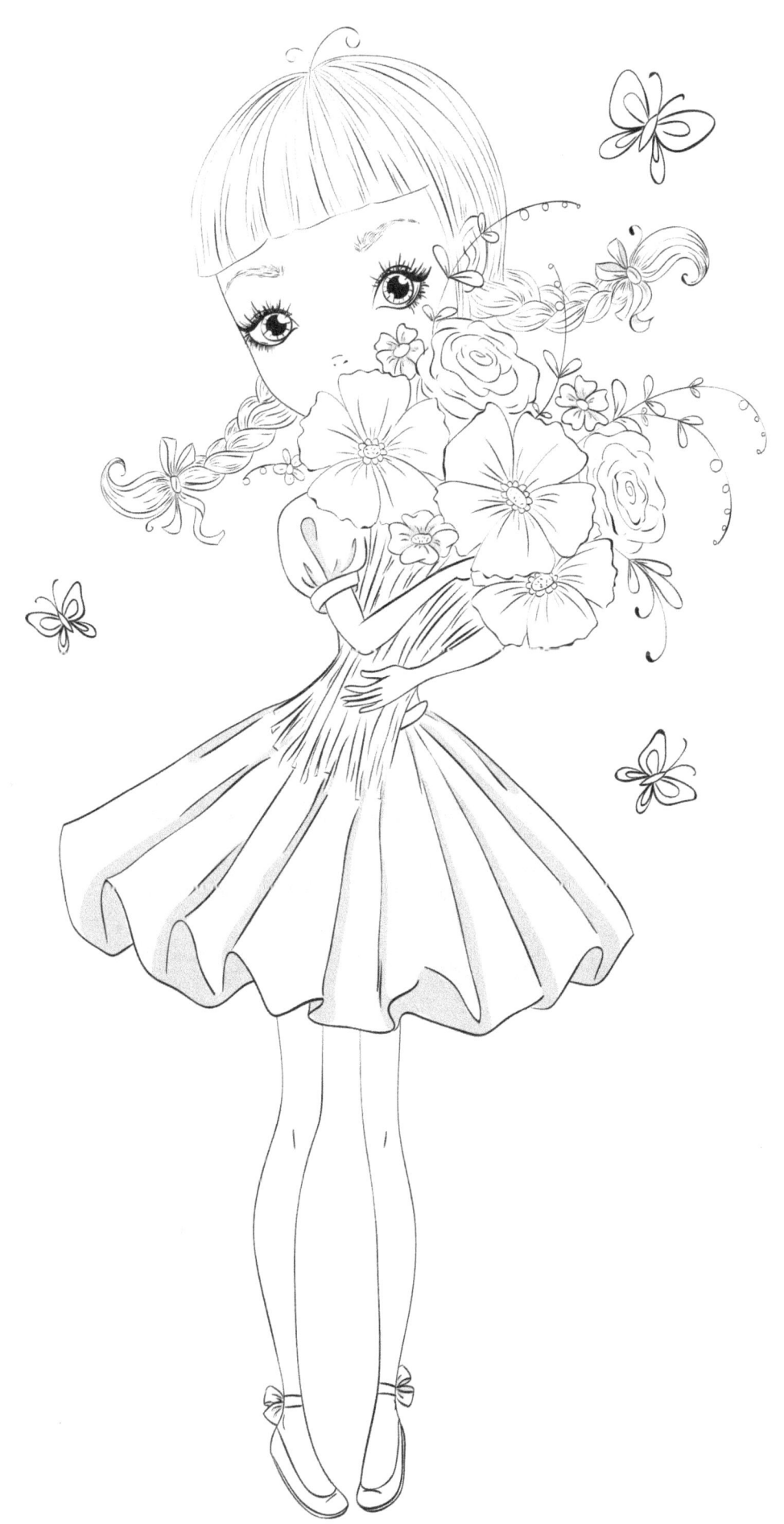

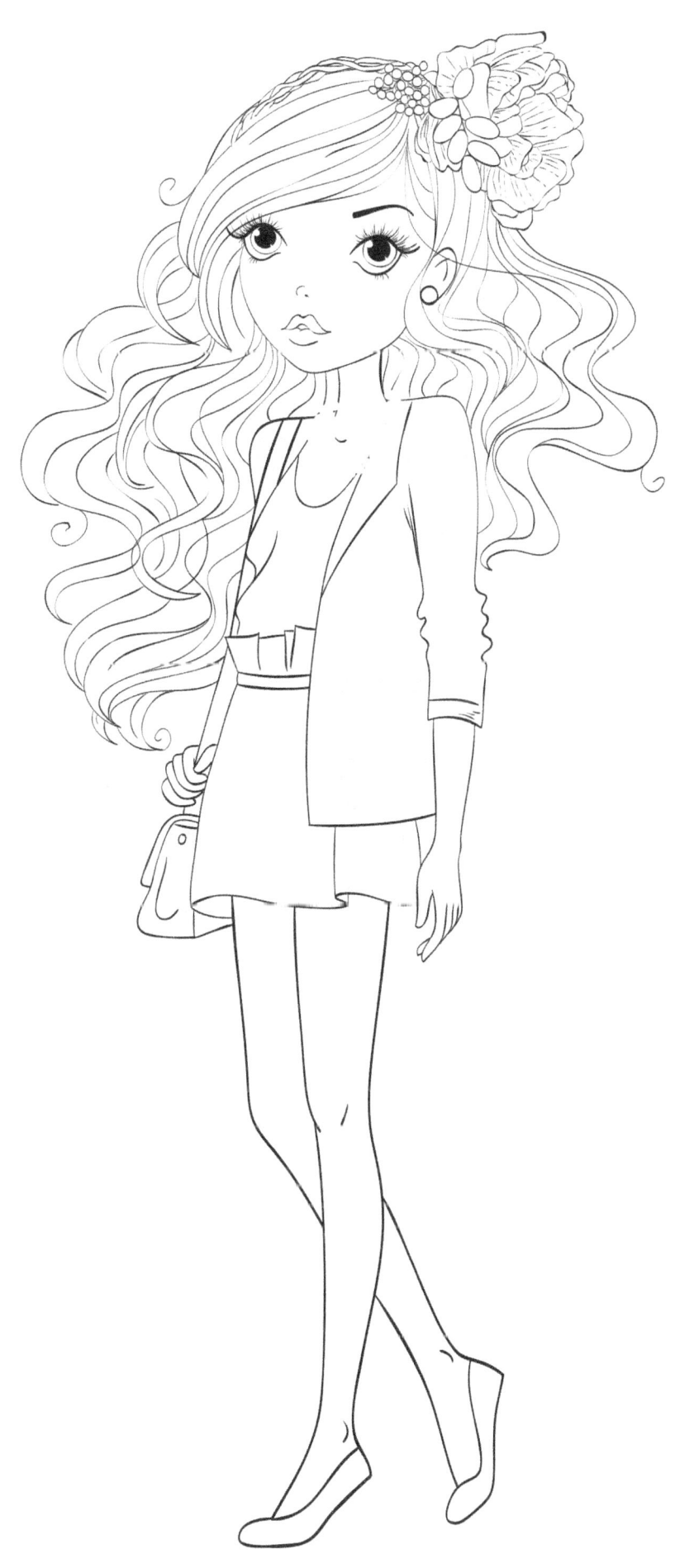

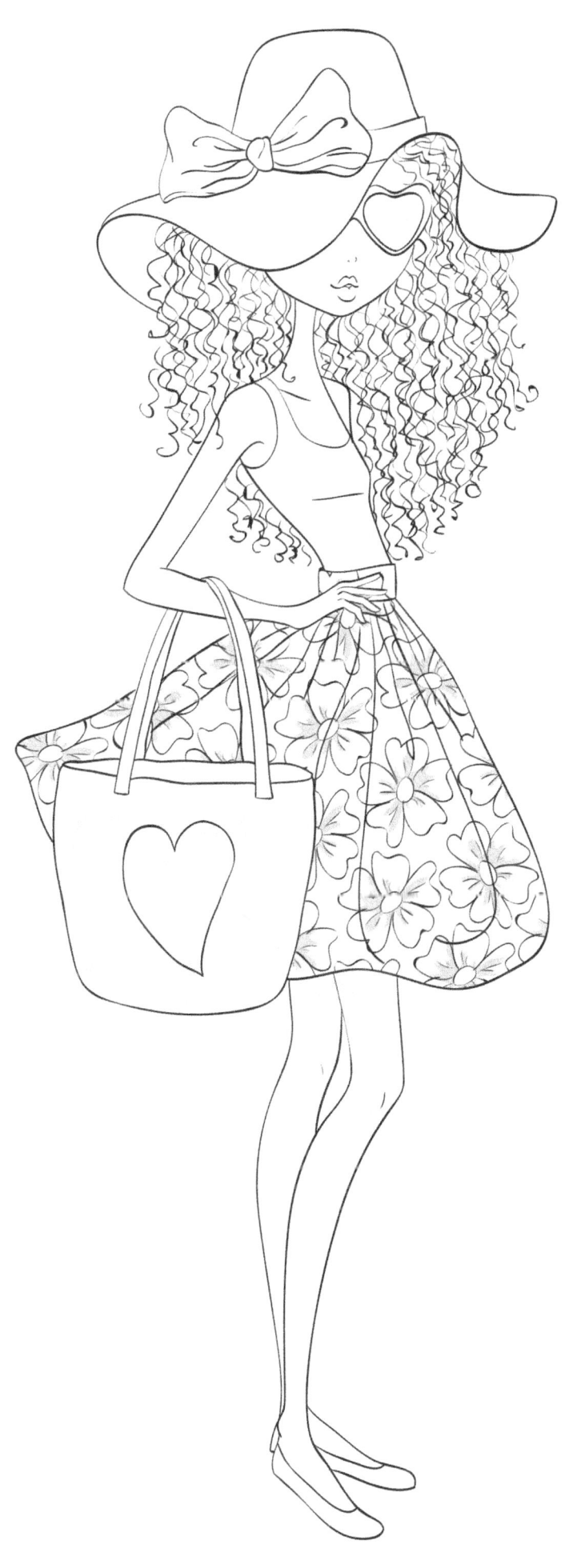

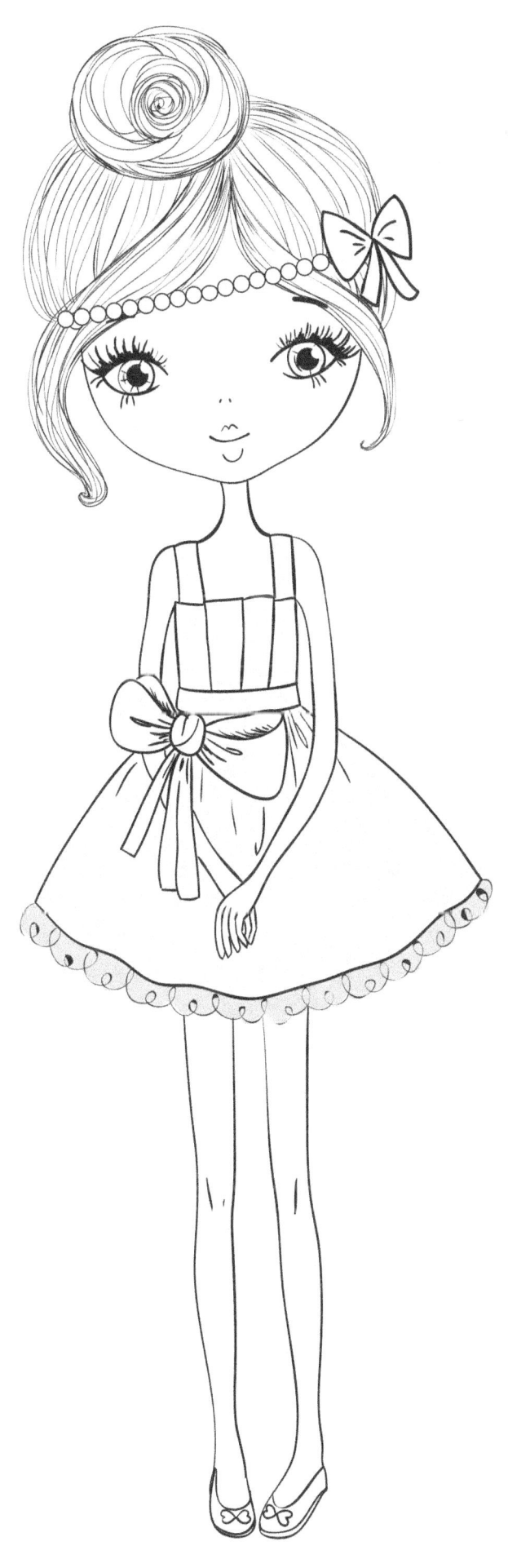

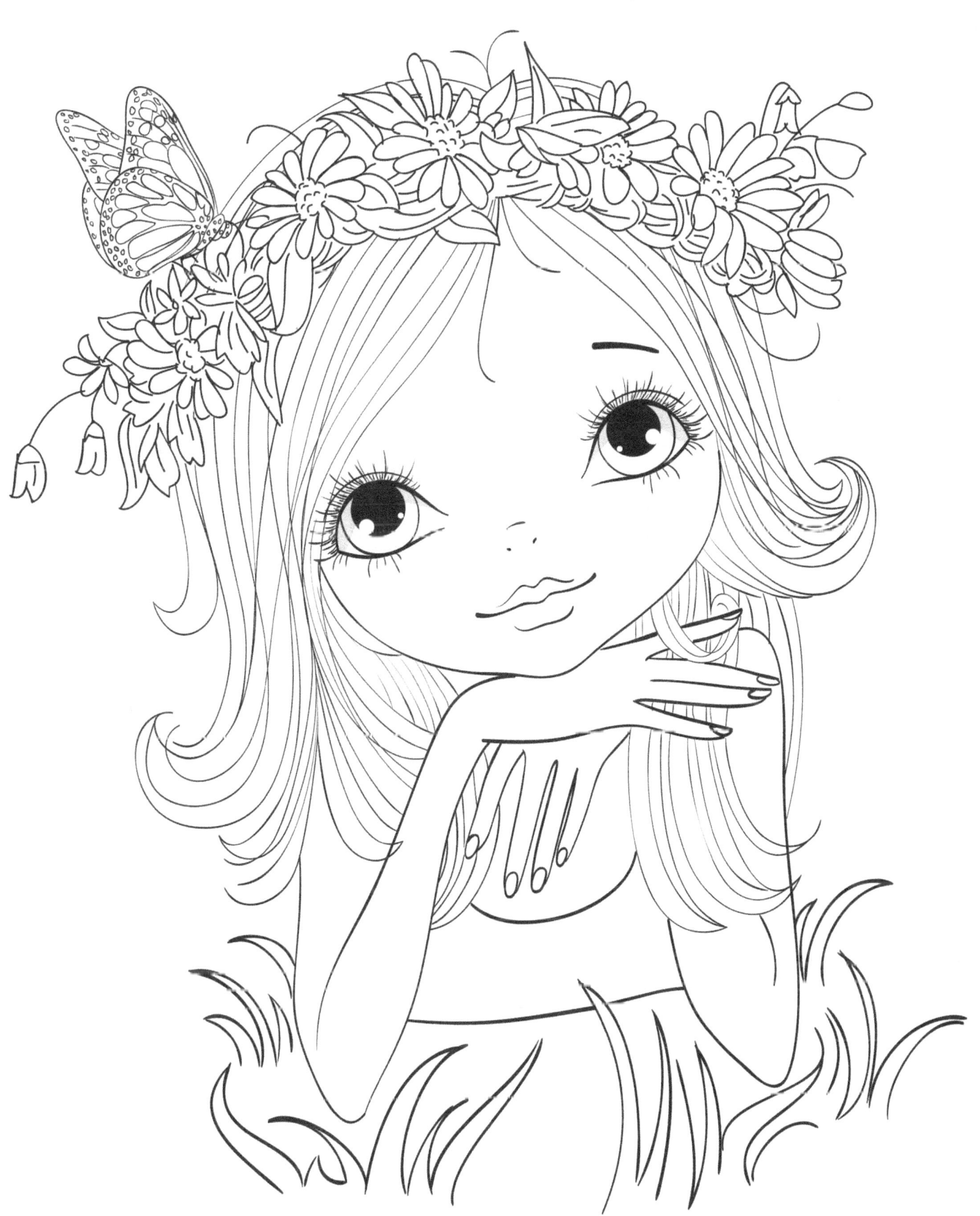

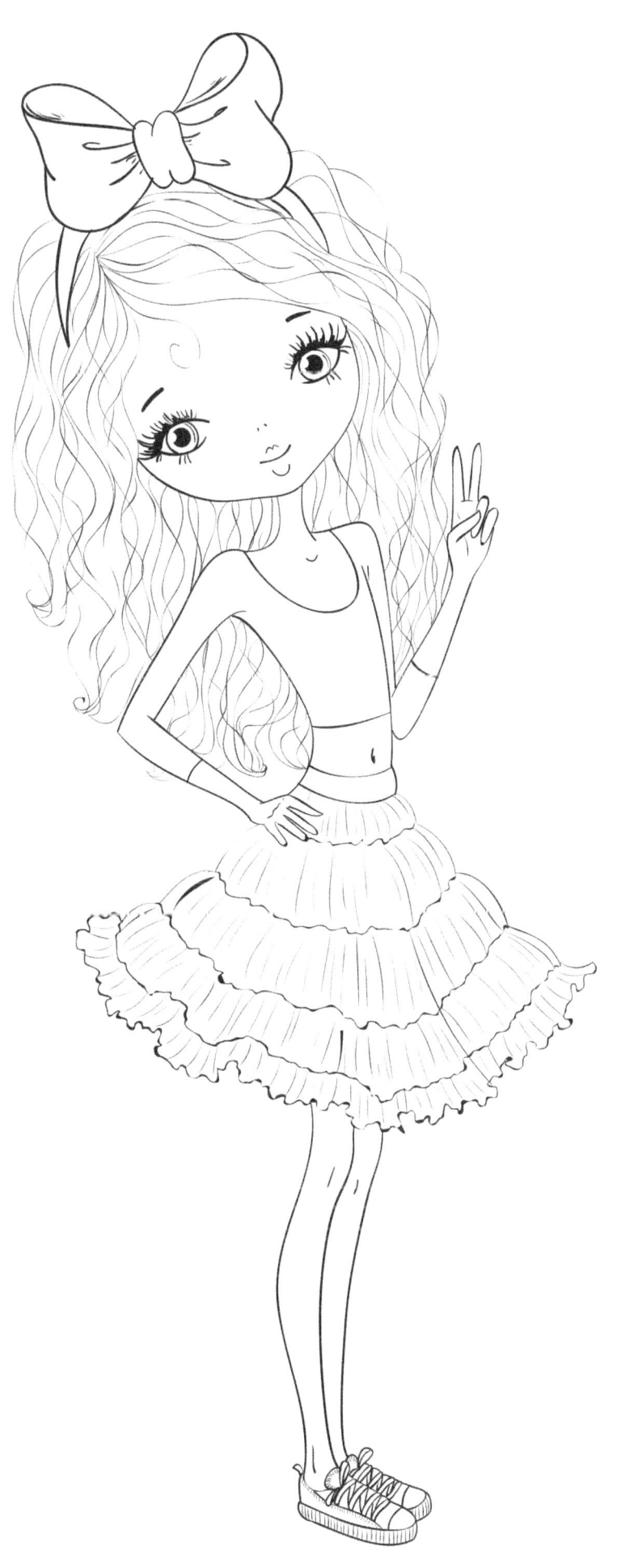

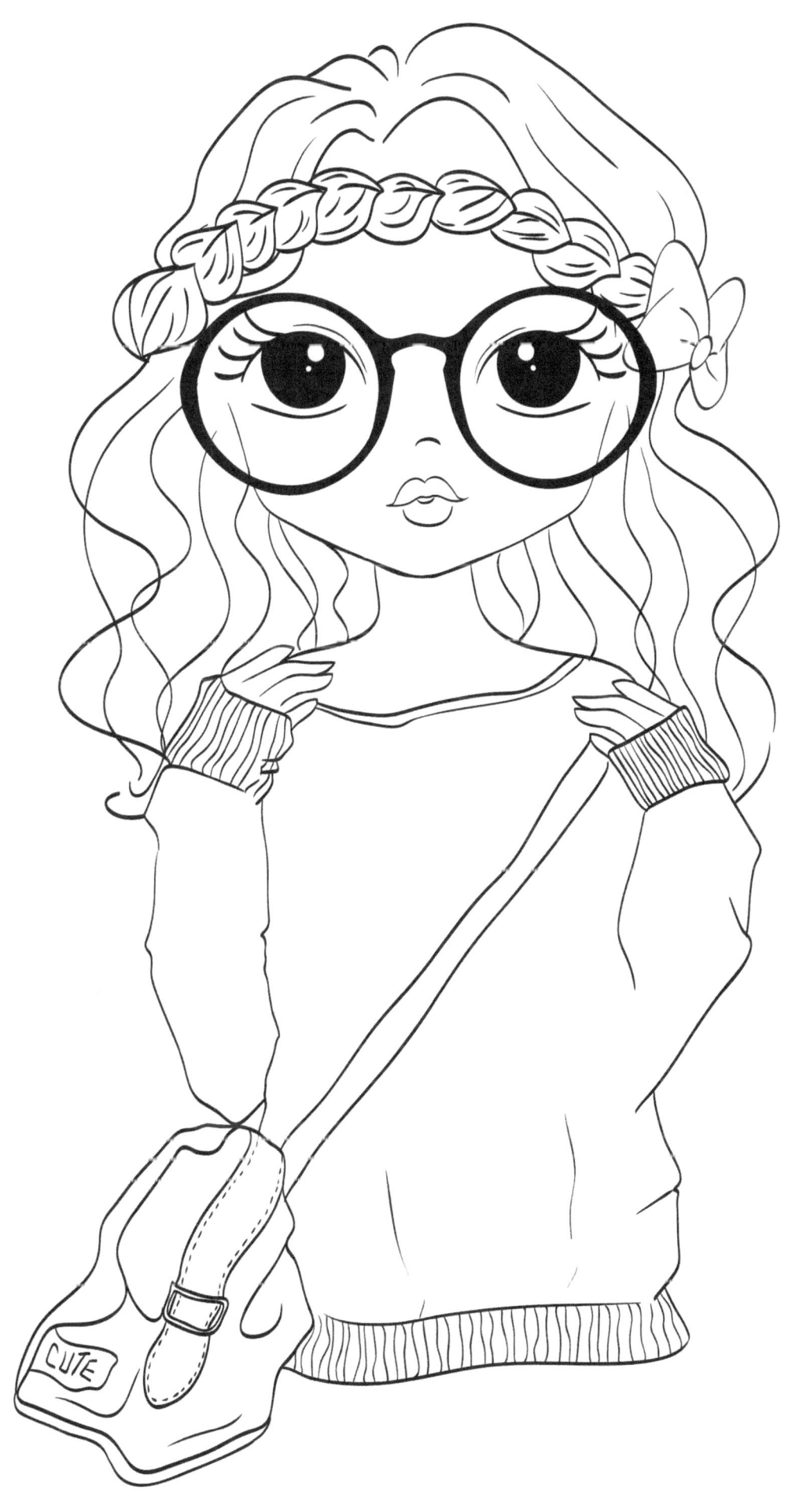

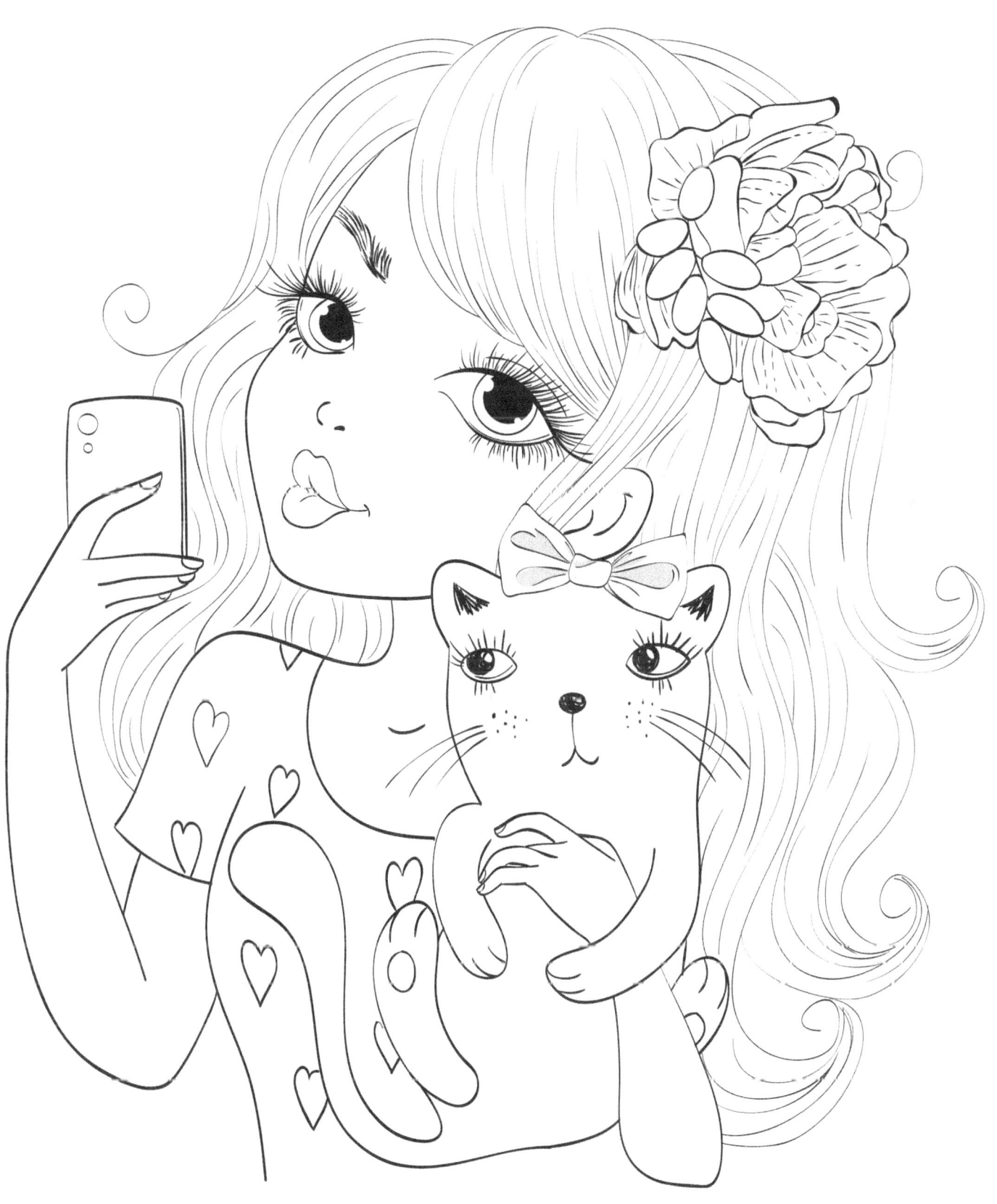

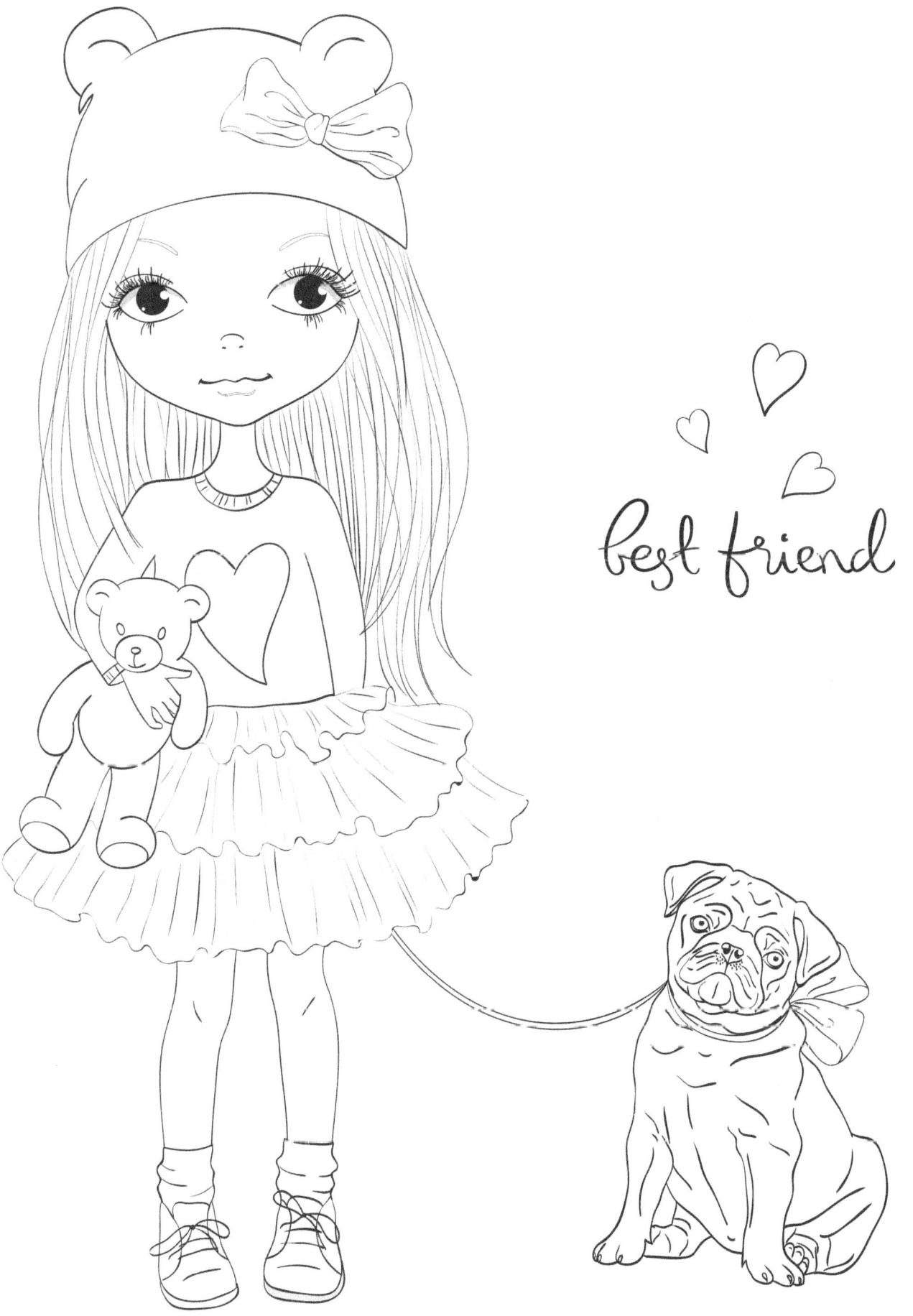

best friend

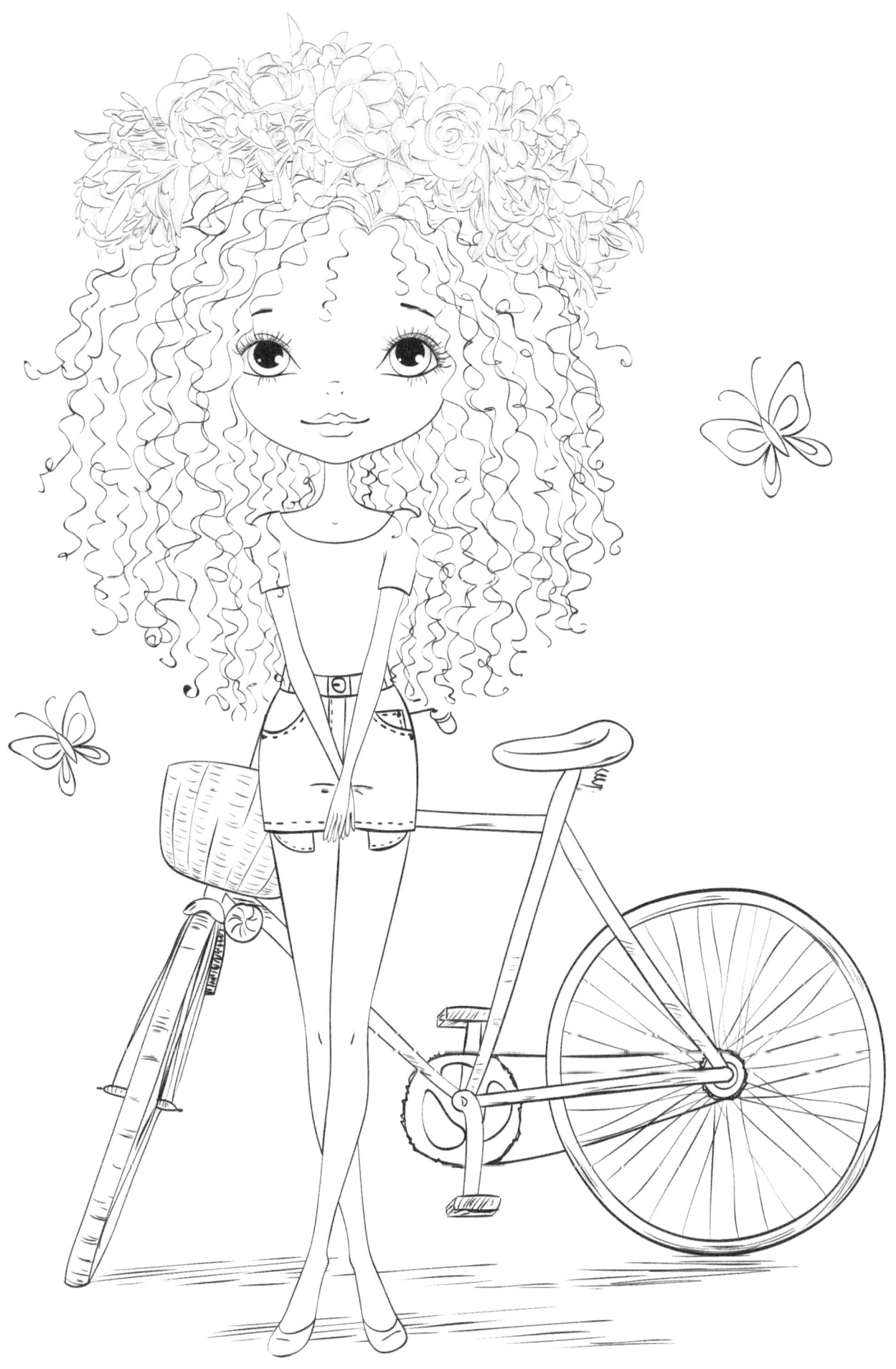

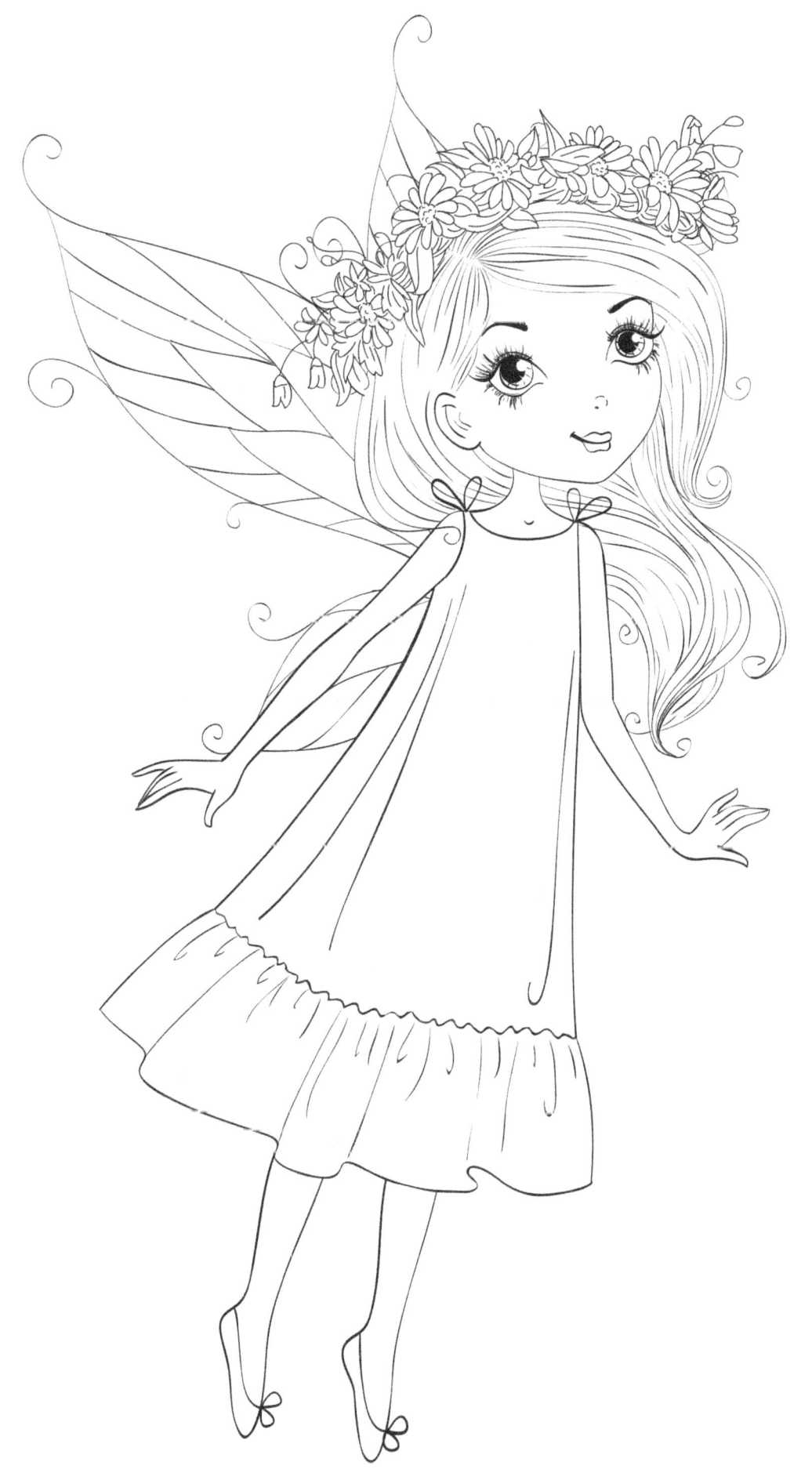

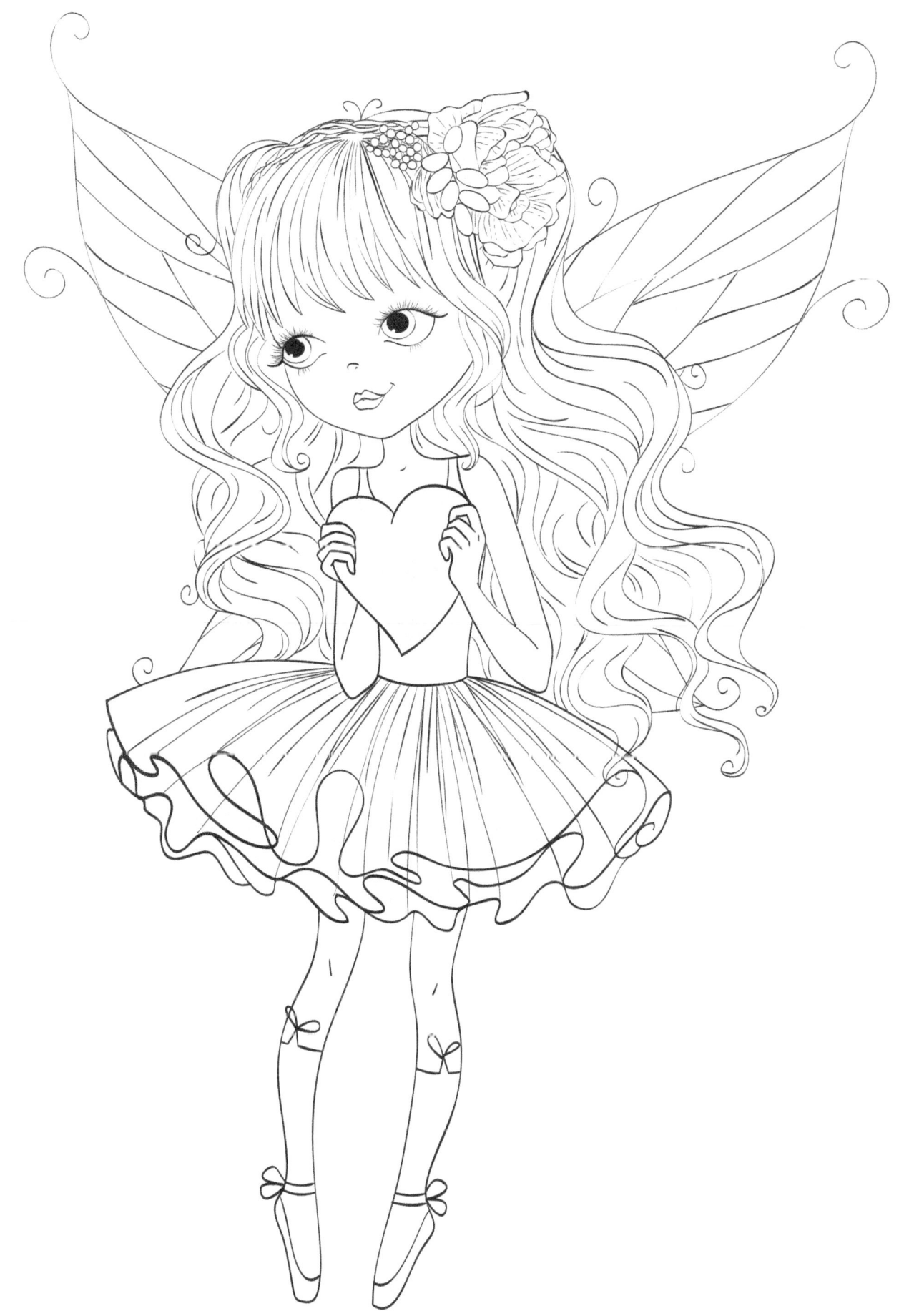

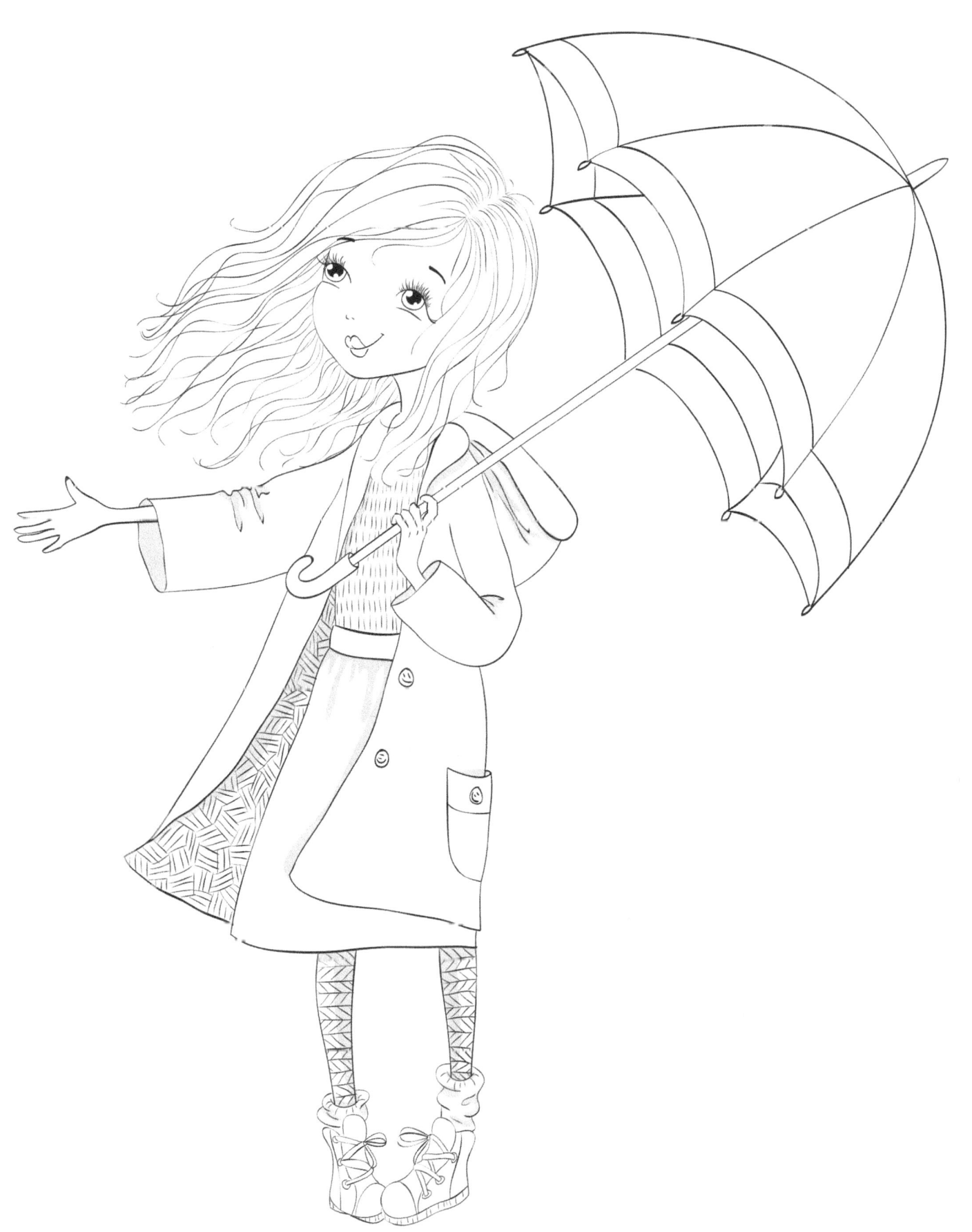

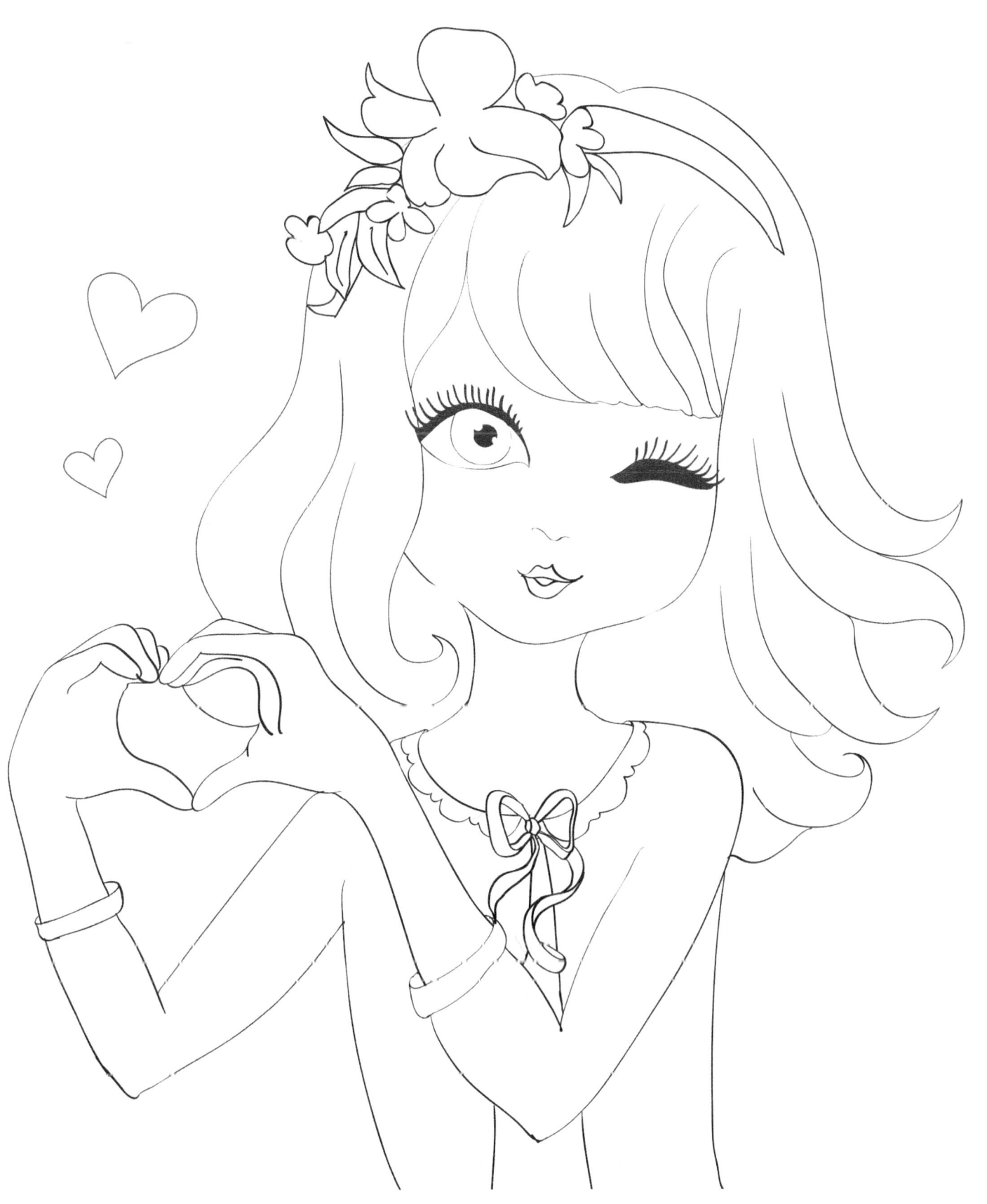

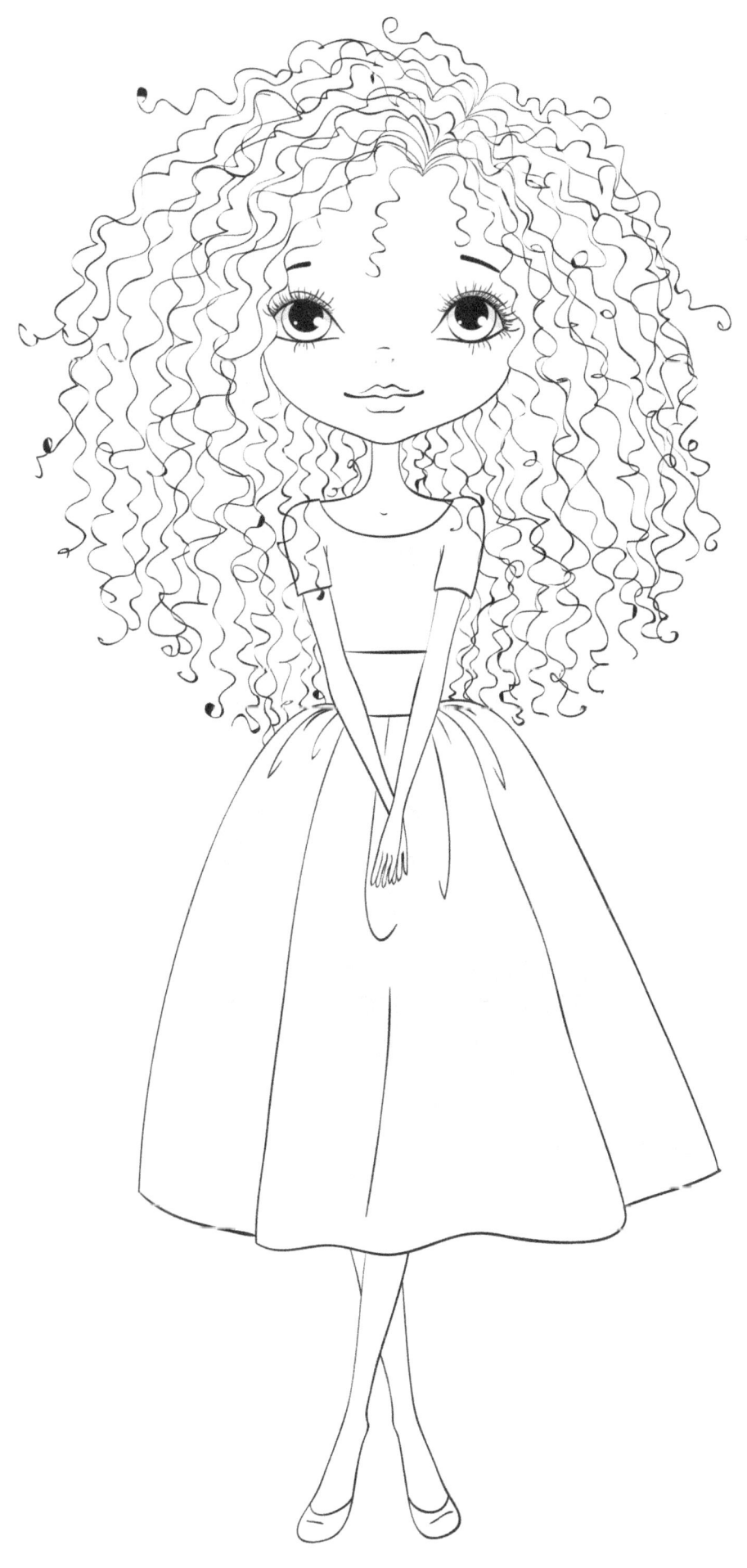

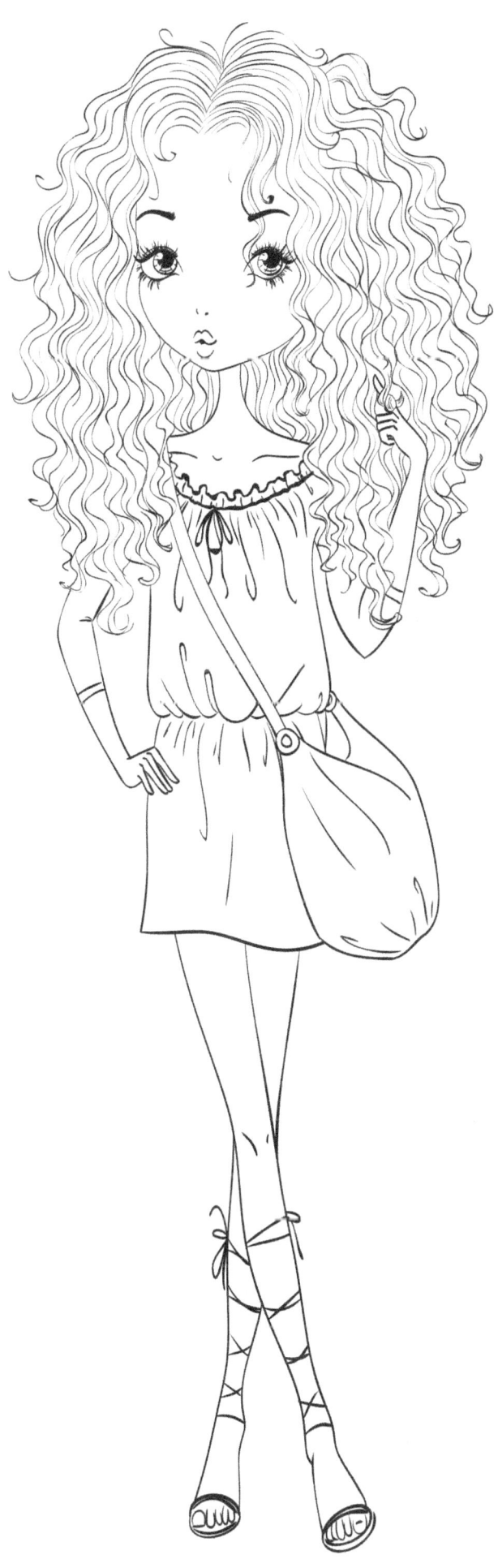

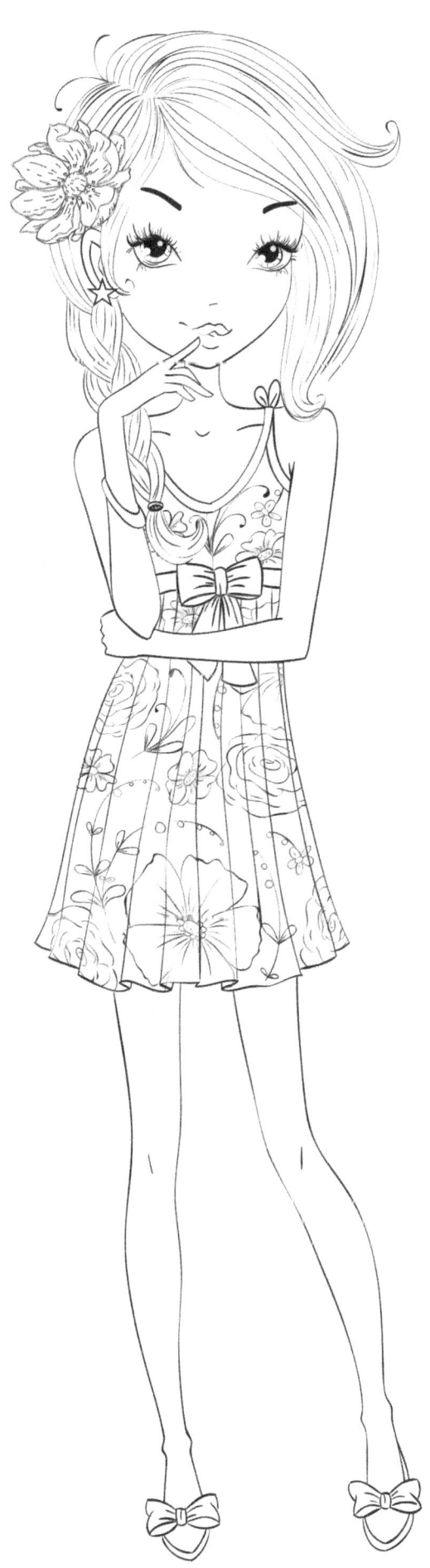

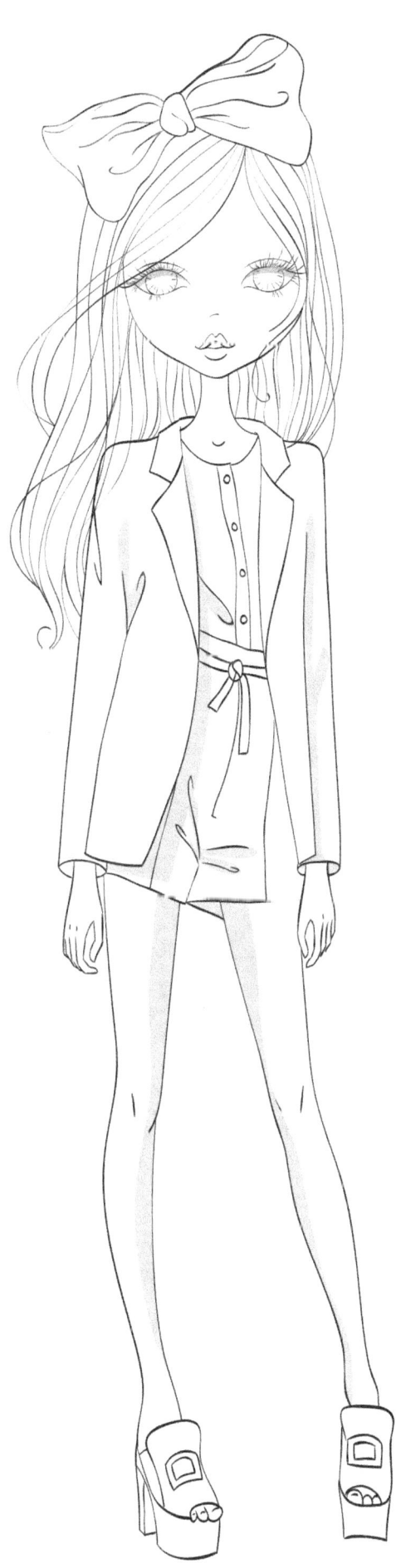

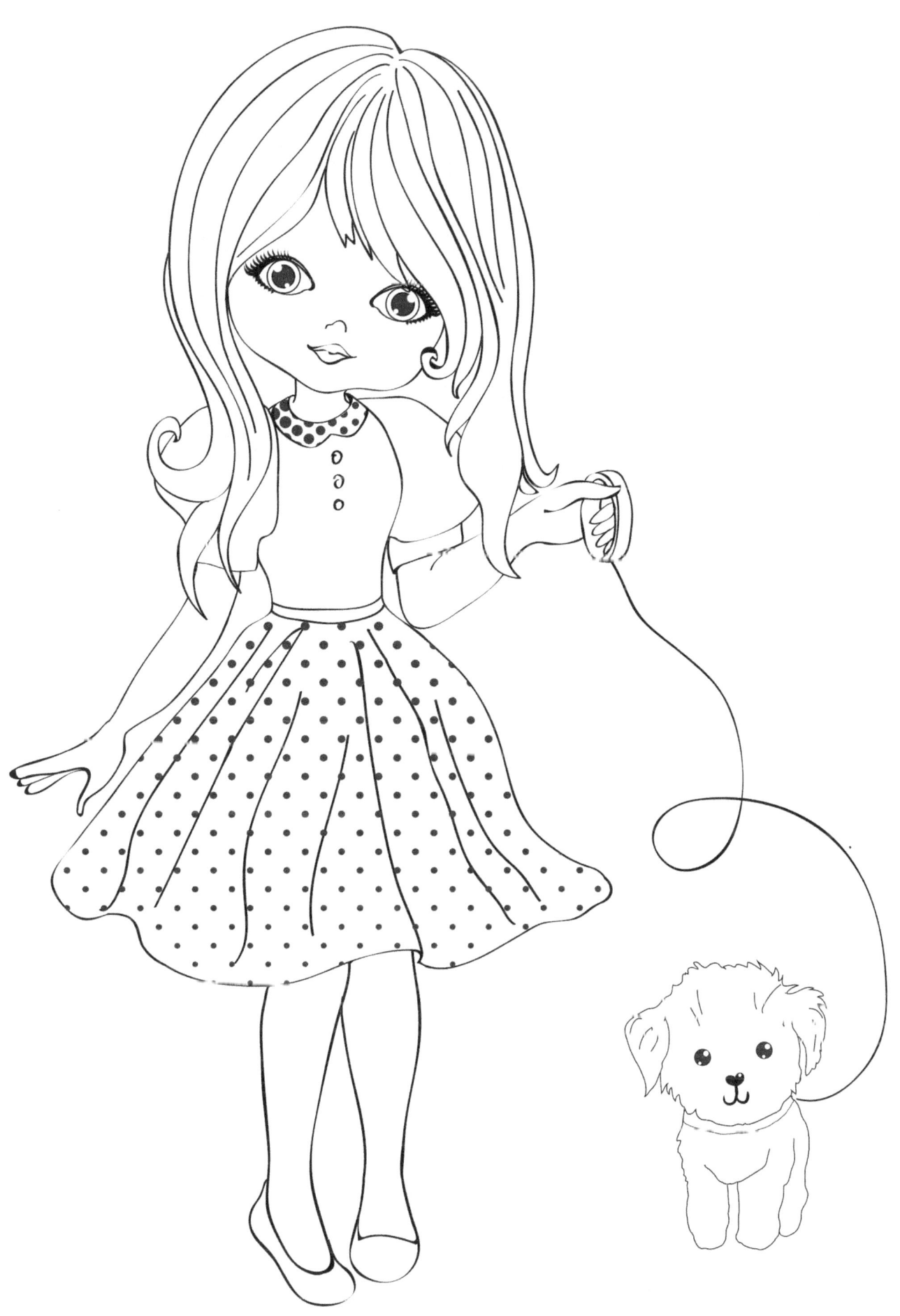

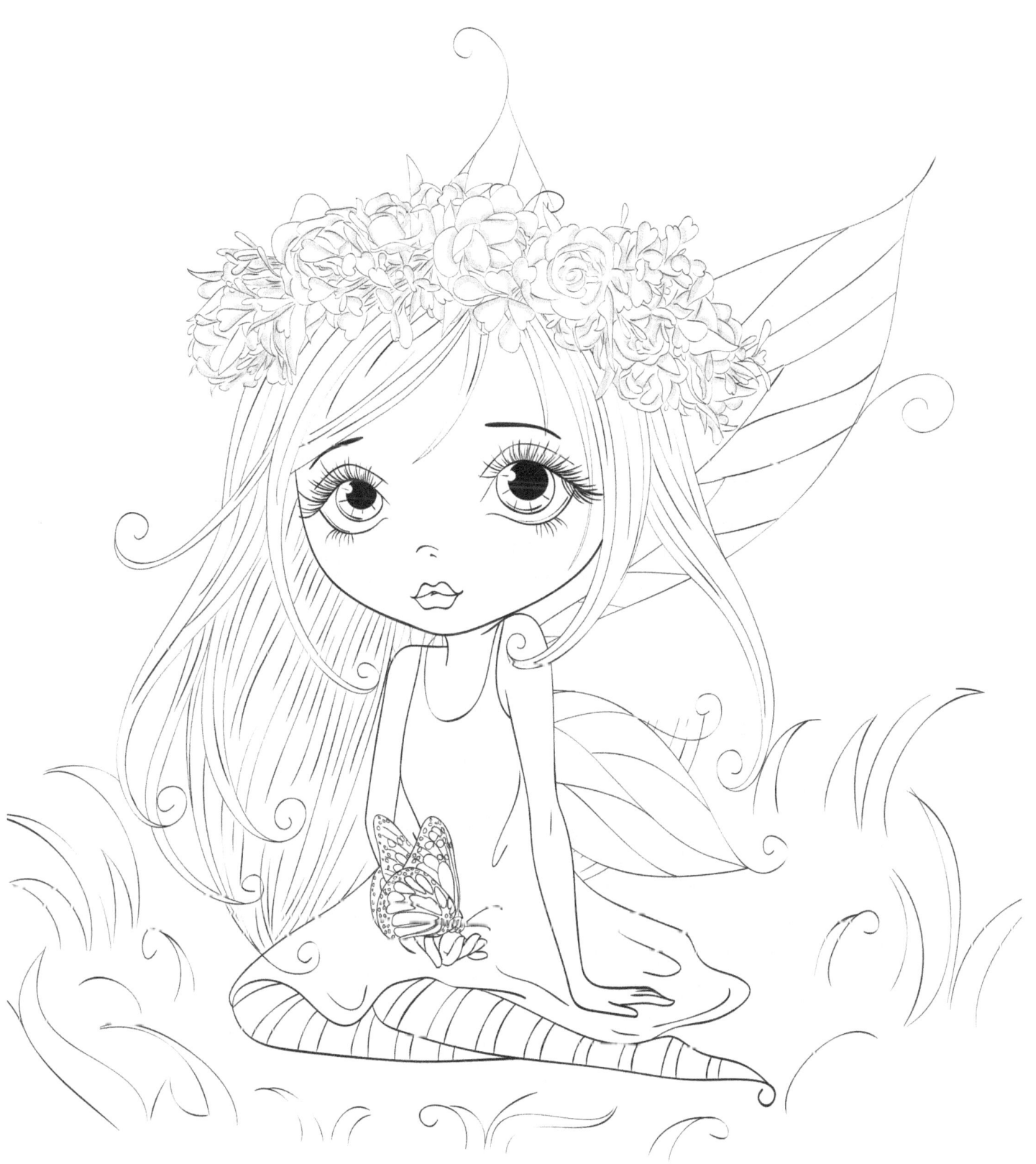

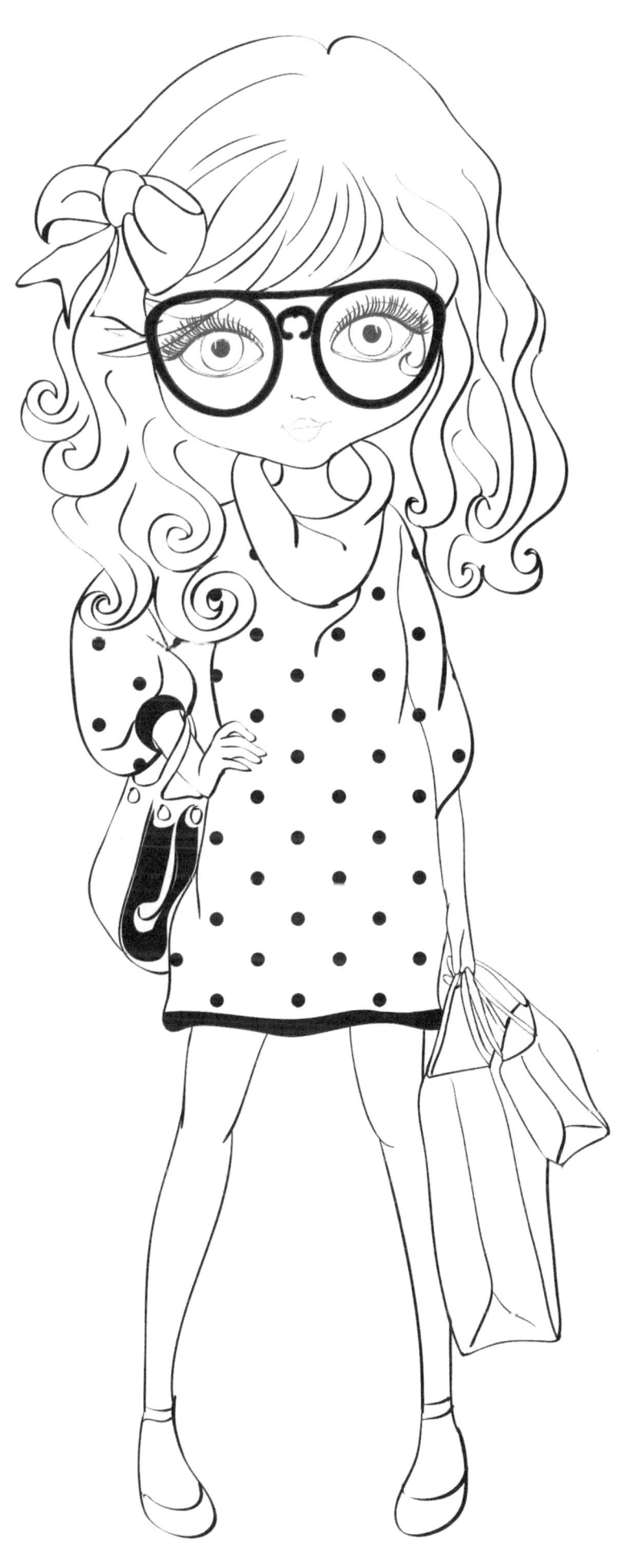

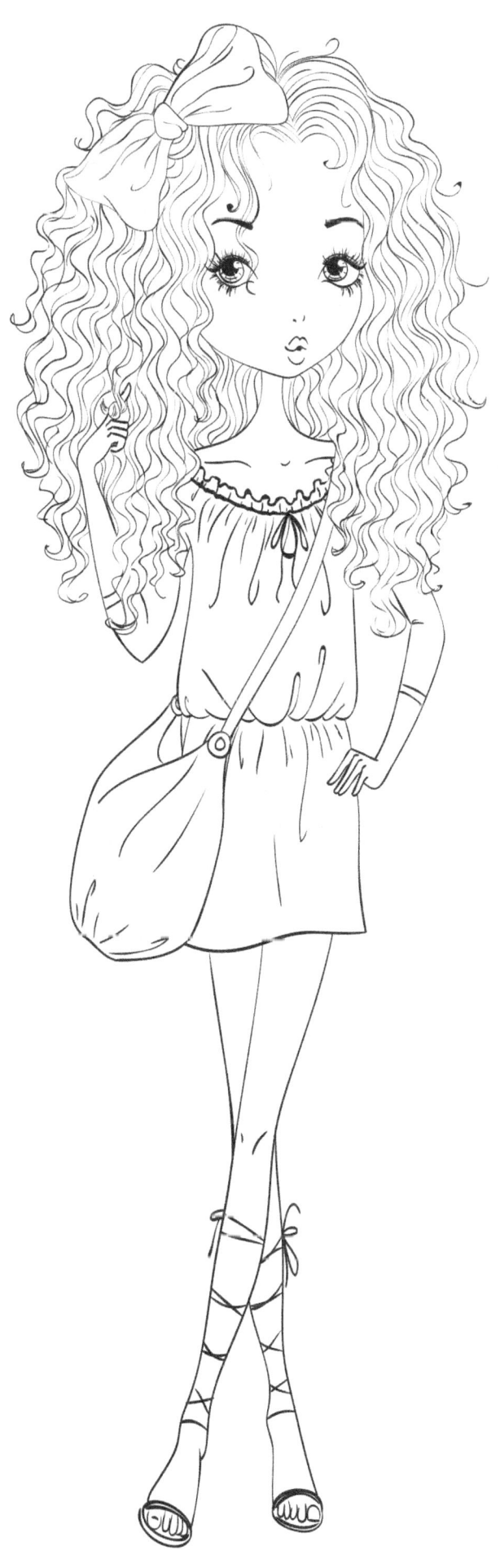

Coloring Book For Girls

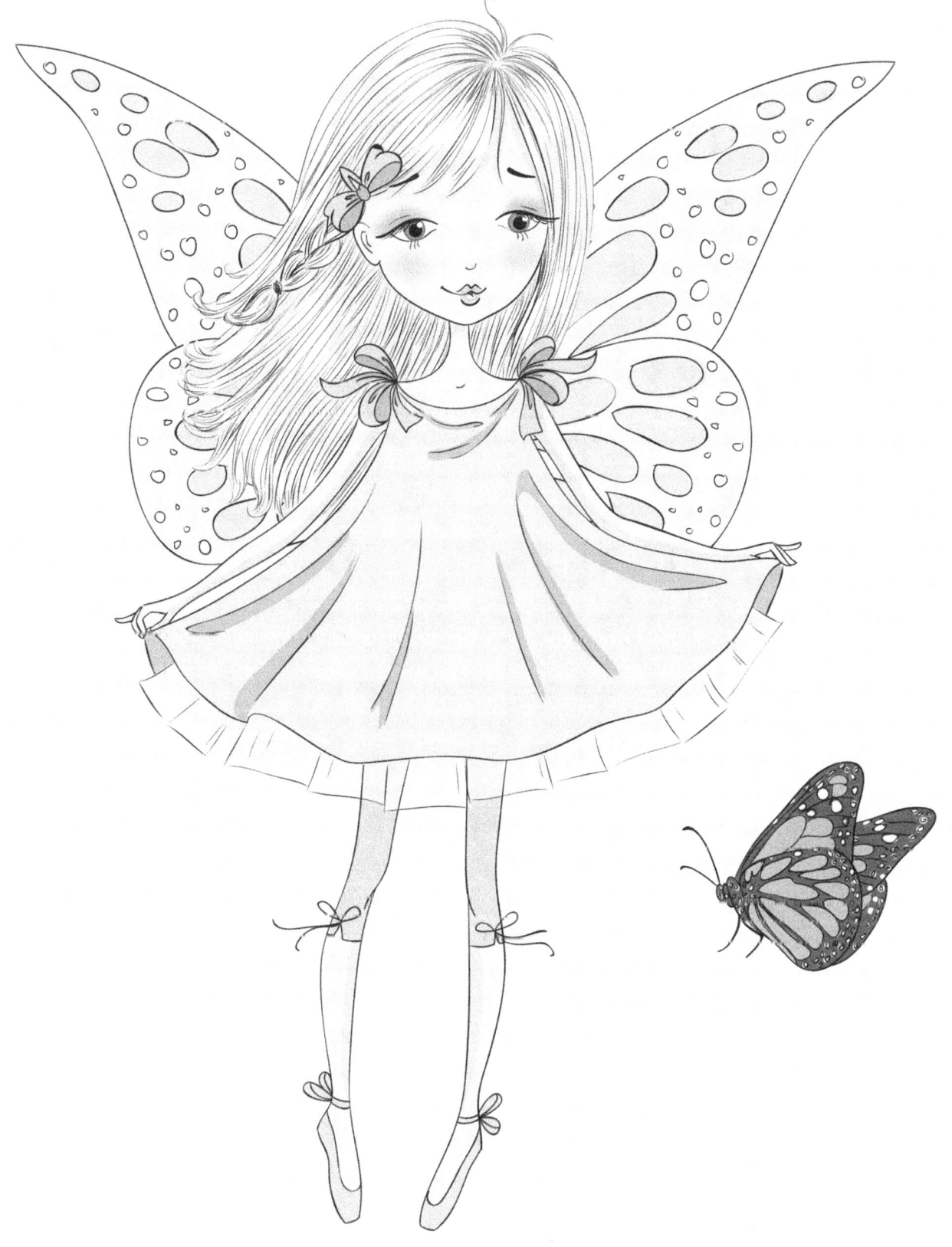

www.ingramcontent.com/pod-product-compliance
Lightning Source LLC
Chambersburg PA
CBHW080133240526
45468CB00009BA/2422